Science History Is No Mystery!

Diane Craig

Consulting Editor, Susan Kosel, M.A. Education

Published by ABDO Publishing Company, 4940 Viking Drive, Edina, Minnesota 55435.

Printed in the United States.

Credits
Edited by: Pam Price
Curriculum Coordinator: Nancy Tuminelly
Cover and Interior Design and Production: Mighty Media
Photo Credits: AbleStock, Brand X Pictures, Comstock, Photodisc, ShutterStock, Stockbyte,
TongRo Image Stock, Wewerka Photography

Library of Congress Cataloging-in-Publication Data

Craig, Diane.
　Science history is no mystery! / Diane Craig.
　　p. cm. -- (Science made simple)
　ISBN 10 1-59928-616-5 (hardcover)
　ISBN 10 1-59928-617-3 (paperback)

　ISBN 13 978-1-59928-616-7 (hardcover)
　ISBN 13 978-1-59928-617-4 (paperback)
　1. Science--History--Juvenile literature. I. Title.

Q126.4.C73 2007
500--dc22

2006022490

SandCastle Level: Transitional

SandCastle™ books are created by a professional team of educators, reading specialists, and content developers around five essential components—phonemic awareness, phonics, vocabulary, text comprehension, and fluency—to assist young readers as they develop reading skills and strategies and increase their general knowledge. All books are written, reviewed, and leveled for guided reading, early reading intervention, and Accelerated Reader® programs for use in shared, guided, and independent reading and writing activities to support a balanced approach to literacy instruction. The SandCastle™ series has four levels that correspond to early literacy development. The levels help teachers and parents select appropriate books for young readers.

Emerging Readers	Beginning Readers	Transitional Readers	Fluent Readers
(no flags)	(1 flag)	(2 flags)	(3 flags)

These levels are meant only as a guide. All levels are subject to change.

The **history** of science shows us how the world has been changed by new ideas, discoveries, and inventions. The ideas of the past are connected to the visions of the future like links in a chain.

Words used to talk about science history:
discovery
fossils
invention

3

Long ago, we thought the earth was flat like a . Now we know it is round like a .

Long ago, we did not know the ☀ was a star. Now we know the moves around the ☀.

Long ago, there were
no . Now
we have and
.

Long ago, we did not have  . Now we can fly around the .

Long ago, we only cooked with . Now we can cook with a .

Long ago, a was bigger than a . Now computers can fit on our laps.

Science History Is No Mystery!

The history of science
is long and complex,
from making tools
to finding fossils of T. rex.

I love learning
science history
so the world is not
a mystery.

Scientists discovered three kinds of matter. They are solid, liquid, and gas. Water is a liquid plants need for growing fast.

A discovery is something you find or figure out. Science is so fun, I just want to shout!

Telling time is important.

First we used sundials.

Later came clocks
and watches.

Then came digital styles.

Technology is changing
faster than ever
because scientists are
so bright and clever!

Science History
Every Day!

We go home when the bell rings at the end of the school day.

What are some inventions you use every day?

18

Some people
need eyeglasses
to see better.

Heather
wears glasses
to help her
see close up.

19

We ride in cars to travel long distances.

People used to ride horses to go from place to place.

Violet uses the Internet to find information about famous scientists.

What are some inventions that you wish for in the future?

Glossary

digital – having or giving a reading that uses the numbers 0 through 9.

discovery – something that is seen or known for the very first time.

fossil – the remains or imprint of something that lived a long time ago.

history – things that happened in the past.

invention – a new thing that is created because someone had the idea to make it. Cars, glasses, and soap were all invented by people.